TULSA CITY-COUNTY LIBRARY

Valentine's Day

Julie Murray

Abdo
HOLIDAYS
Kids

abdopublishing.com

Published by Abdo Kids, a division of ABDO, PO Box 398166, Minneapolis, Minnesota 55439.
Copyright © 2018 by Abdo Consulting Group, Inc. International copyrights reserved in all countries.
No part of this book may be reproduced in any form without written permission from the publisher.

Printed in the United States of America, North Mankato, Minnesota.

102017

012018

 THIS BOOK CONTAINS
RECYCLED MATERIALS

Photo Credits: Glow Images, iStock, Shutterstock

Production Contributors: Teddy Borth, Jennie Forsberg, Grace Hansen

Design Contributors: Christina Doffing, Candice Keimig, Dorothy Toth

Publisher's Cataloging in Publication Data

Names: Murray, Julie, author.

Title: Valentine's day / by Julie Murray.

Description: Minneapolis, Minnesota : Abdo Kids, 2018. | Series: Holidays |
    Includes glossary, index and online resource (page 24).

Identifiers: LCCN 2017942867 | ISBN 9781532103957 (lib.bdg.) | ISBN 9781532105074 (ebook) |
    ISBN 9781532105630 (Read-to-me ebook)

Subjects: LCSH: Holidays--Juvenile literature. | Valentine's Day--Juvenile literature. |
    Celebrations--Juvenile literature.

Classification: DDC 394.2618--dc23

LC record available at https://lccn.loc.gov/2017942867

Table of Contents

Valentine's Day

February 14th is Valentine's Day! It is a day about love.

We show love in many ways.

Anna gives her dad a card.

She hugs him.

Sam wrote a **poem**.

He tells it to Ellie.

Tyler gives his mom flowers.

She loves them!

Lily opens a box of chocolates.

Yum!

15

Beth made heart cookies.

She **shares** them.

The kids have a party. They pass out valentines.

Grace loves Valentine's Day!

Signs of Valentine's Day

box of chocolates

cards

flowers

heart cookies

Glossary

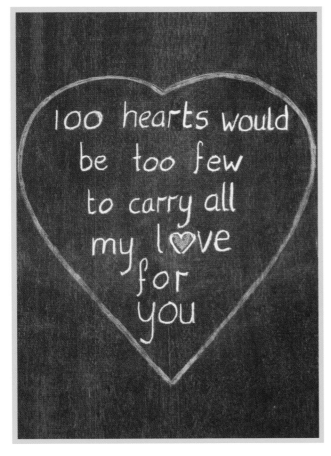

poem
written word that usually has a
rhythm and creates feeling.

share
to kindly use or enjoy a thing
with others.

Index

Abdo Kids
ONLINE
FREE! ONLINE MULTIMEDIA RESOURCES

Visit **abdokids.com** and use this code to access crafts, games, videos, and more!

Abdo Kids Code:
HVK3957